Land of the ZEBRA

by Jocelyn Arundel

Created and Published by
The National Wildlife Federation
Washington, D.C.

ZEBRAS AND GIRAFFES ARE AMAZING

The zebra's frequent companion, the giraffe, is the **TALLEST ANIMAL IN THE WORLD.** An adult zebra could walk under the giraffe's stomach; and weighs only about a third as much as his towering friend. Even a baby giraffe is taller than the zebra.

Most zebras are striped, but take a close look —no zebra's **STRIPES** exactly match another's.

The zebra actually *is* a striped **HORSE**. The name of his family is *equidae* (EK-wa- dee) — which comes from the Latin word — *equus* — for domesticated horse.

Where you find zebras, you are sure to find **WATER.** Other animals, knowing this, follow.

The gentle giraffes have truly **BIG HEARTS:** they're two feet long!

From horn to hoof, a male **GIRAFFE may measure EIGHTEEN FEET.** Most **ZEBRAS** —shoulder to toe— **are seldom as much as FIVE FEET tall.**

The giraffe has a **SIX-FOOT-LONG NECK** with only seven bones in it— same number a mouse has— but much longer! His legs are long, too; so to drink he does the split.

Lucky giraffe–his **EIGHTEEN INCH TONGUE** can reach out and wrap a-round anything he might want to eat, even high branches of acacias.

5

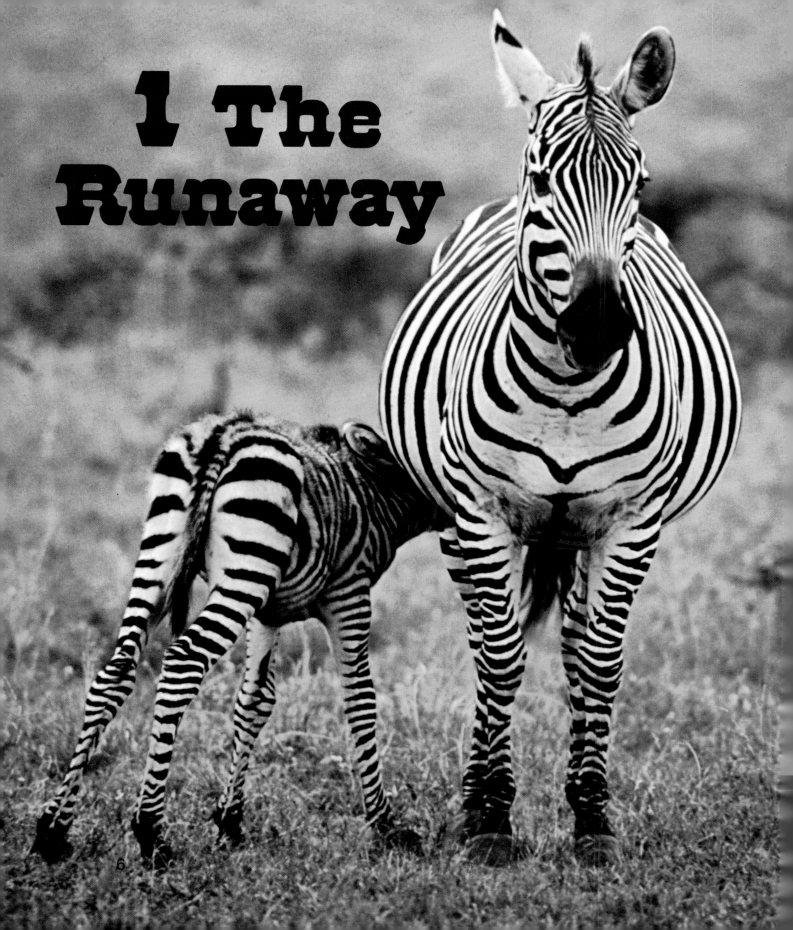

1 The Runaway

"Kwa-Kwa!" The alarm suddenly sounded. Neck stretched and nostrils flared, the zebra sentinel sniffed and snorted, and again sounded his alarm for all to hear.

The herd wheeled and sped away across the plain, with little Chief in their midst. Their hoofs pounded noisily on the hard-packed earth. Clouds of dust billowed into the air.

Chief was terrified. He was afraid of the animal which was attacking them, whatever it might be. He was afraid, too, of the sharp zebra hoofs kicking up from the ground right in front of him and of the thundering mass that was pressing down on him from behind.

He no longer ran on the edge of the herd, protected by his mother from the crushing stampede. He was too old for that. But at scarcely a year, he still feared that he might fall and be crushed. Perhaps he would run too slowly and be pushed. Perhaps he would stumble over a foal, a baby, that had been caught up in the sudden swirl of zebras.

Chief's heart was pounding. His lungs were beginning to give out. He

A fuzzy little filly contentedly drinks mother's nourishing milk.

would soon be out of breath, and might be trampled.

Then suddenly, almost as suddenly as they had begun, the herd ended their mad dash. Weary and panting, Chief turned to look back. He saw no fearsome creature. There was no lion, no leopard, no jackal, no hyena. Perhaps it had been a false alarm. There were many. Or perhaps there had been real trouble and they had outrun the hungry enemy.

Slowly, the herd filed back to the pond where they had been drinking. They scarcely glanced at an animal hurrying away. But Chief looked, and he shuddered. It was a lion, with the foal it had caught that was too young and too weak to keep up with the rest of the herd.

Chief did not follow the others. He turned away. This was a difficult life. Why not strike out on his own? Surely he could find a new and better way to live. There must be some place where there were no lions and where he would not have to spend his days caught in wild stampedes.

Perhaps Fuzz, the downy-haired little female with whom he galloped over the plains, would go with him. He called, but Fuzz didn't answer. Fuzz was drinking her mother's milk. She was too young to leave home.

Newly born and still wet, a zebra foal raises his head.

Chief began walking away. "Kwa-ha-ha!" Someone was calling. This time it was not an alarm. It was Chief's father beckoning.

The colt paused. Perhaps he should go back. But no, his mind was made up. Chief trotted briskly away. He was determined.

A hundred yards farther, beside an acacia tree now nearly bare of leaves, Chief spied a mare lying on her side. He recognized her as one of his father's harem. This, then was why his father had been barking.

Before Chief could investigate, something wonderful happened. Two tiny black hoofs appeared and then a head, shaped just like Chief's, but much smaller. Soon, it was all there—a brand new foal, a perfect miniature zebra. The young runaway stood fascinated. He did not know it, but it was as though he were looking at his own first hours.

The mare slicked down the rough coat of the baby with its ripples of chocolate brown stripes. The stripes would darken with age, but their special pattern would never change. The stripes wouldn't be like Chief's or anyone else's. They would be the foal's own, like fingerprints.

With her soft, dark muzzle, the mare nudged her little one to his feet. The foal was eager to stand. Like any newborn, it had extra-long legs. The extra inches were important. The legs would carry the small body almost as fast as an adult's. But just now, they were weak and wobbly.

Chief wanted to leave, but he didn't. He watched the newborn

In minutes, he struggles to his feet.

scrambling to get up. Soon, teetering, it stood beside its mother and began to nurse.

All at once, there was a whirring. The sound came from above. Chief looked up. A vulture was soaring overhead on huge wings, twice as wide from tip to tip as Chief was tall.

Success! He stands on wobbly legs now, beside his mother, gazing at Africa's vast fields of sunlit savanna grass lying before him.

The bird swooped down. Somewhere nearby an animal had made a kill. It was growing dark and there would be more trouble. Chief had best be on his way.

The night was cold and scary. A mouse scurried through the dry grass. A dog bayed. A hyena found food and laughed. Even the wind whistling through the ant galls, the hollow swellings on the thornbushes, made Chief shudder.

The first flush of dawn was a welcome sight. So were the giraffes silently pruning the bushes. They would watch for trouble. Chief whinnied with pleasure and began to graze on the red oat grass. A wildebeest had already helped himself to the leaves, but Chief didn't mind.

10

A frisky colt's frolicking sends a flock of egrets exploding skyward.

He knew that the leftover wiry stems were really much tastier.

Now, from down in a hollow, a whole herd of wildebeest appeared, whirling, bounding, snorting.

A bull leaped and bucked playfully around Chief until the colt could take no more. He galloped off past a young foal nuzzling its mother, and he frightened into flight a flock of egrets feeding near them in the field.

The day was hot, and each day after was hotter still. Occasional clouds played in the sky, but there

Love is . . . standing side by side.

was no rain. The daily water was getting harder and harder to find.

What had once been a broad pond was now a mud flat and a sea of birds—storks and spoonbills—come to nest. There was no longer enough water to drink. But Chief found a good well in a dry riverbed. Some clever elephant had dug the hole.

There were other surprises. One day a huge bird, bigger than all the ones on the mud flat, blocked Chief's way. She was a billow of plumes set on long, pink legs, an ostrich twice as tall, almost, as Chief. Chief kept his distance. The ostrich could run as fast as he and, if angered, could kick him badly.

11

Chief's daily search for water took him, at last, into the woodlands at the edge of the savanna. A happy throng of baboons dropped down out of the trees and hurried by, squealing and chattering. But toward dusk, Chief heard a different kind of scream, and then he saw a leopard carrying its prey up into a tree.

There were dangers everywhere Chief went. He hadn't left his troubles behind. He had left his friends.

Chief stayed near the woods because here was water. But when he saw dark clouds bunched together on the horizon, he set out to return to the open plains.

Soon the air was filled with the thunder of rainstorms and of great hordes of animals. Chief wasn't the only one going back to the savanna. There were streams of zebras pouring like rivers onto the newly wet plain. Chief came upon two stallions jousting, and was filled with joy.

Chief found a young stallion and charged at him playfully. They reared and lashed out with hoofs then, tired of fighting, grazed peacefully, shoulder to shoulder.

**Mature stallions battle eagerly.
To the winner will go all the mares.**

Zebras and impalas share the plains, grazing in peace. Then, of a sudden, sensing trouble, the impalas test the air and flee.

Other young stallions joined Chief and his friend. But as they grew older, the bouts grew more fierce. Soon, they had become battles. Chief was ready to use his fighting skills to attack stallions of harem herds so that he could steal away their mares and foals. But as often as he tried, he lost.

Then something happened that gave Chief his big chance. One afternoon, the zebras were on the plain grazing with a herd of impalas. A whiff of trouble floated in on the wind. The antelopes raised their heads and listened intently.

Ears forward, neck up, Chief tested the air for danger. His nostrils flared.

Then he snorted a warning. Others snorted in response. A pack of wild dogs was approaching.

These were killers. They worked as a team. At top speed they would outrace Chief or any of his friends. Some would press hard, yapping and snapping at the flying hoofs. Others would lag behind, waiting for one animal to leave the herd or fall away.

Chief and his companions broke into sudden flight. Other herds nearby joined the stampede. Chief,

Wild dogs hound zebras into flight.

now swift and sure of himself, did not hesitate to gallop in their midst. There was no danger that he would be trampled. His zebra heart was strong and well-developed. So were the spacious lungs that would keep him abreast of the others. But in a matter of minutes, he and all the other zebras would be winded.

The wild dogs followed close, howling their hunting cry. Then, the dogs turned away to chase a zebra in another herd.

In the stampede, four fillies, young mares, split away from their group. Chief followed eagerly.

15

After a hard day's run, there's nothing like a drink at the water hole.

This time there would be no fierce battle, no biting, no flailing of hoofs. Chief was lucky.

He moved in quickly to claim his fillies. With gentle nips, he turned them toward open country, where a broad expanse of grass beckoned. Chief looked the field over with a practiced eye. He listened with an attentive ear. He sniffed with a sensitive nose.

There were dangers in this country, Chief knew. But there were dangers in every country, and Chief would keep watch. If there was trouble, he would run swiftly and lead his mares to safety.

They grazed contentedly and then, toward evening, Chief led them to a water hole. This, too, he checked. Then, he sounded the all clear. Eagerly pushing and shoving, his fillies moved in and drank their fill. Now, back they went to the grass to graze.

Chief enjoyed the excitement. He was strong and experienced, now. If charged by a lion or challenged by a rival, he could protect his herd, he was sure.

In years to come the herd would grow. To his mares would be born colts and fillies. It would be a big herd . . . and a good life.

At sunset, zebras and ostriches welcome the evening's cool air.

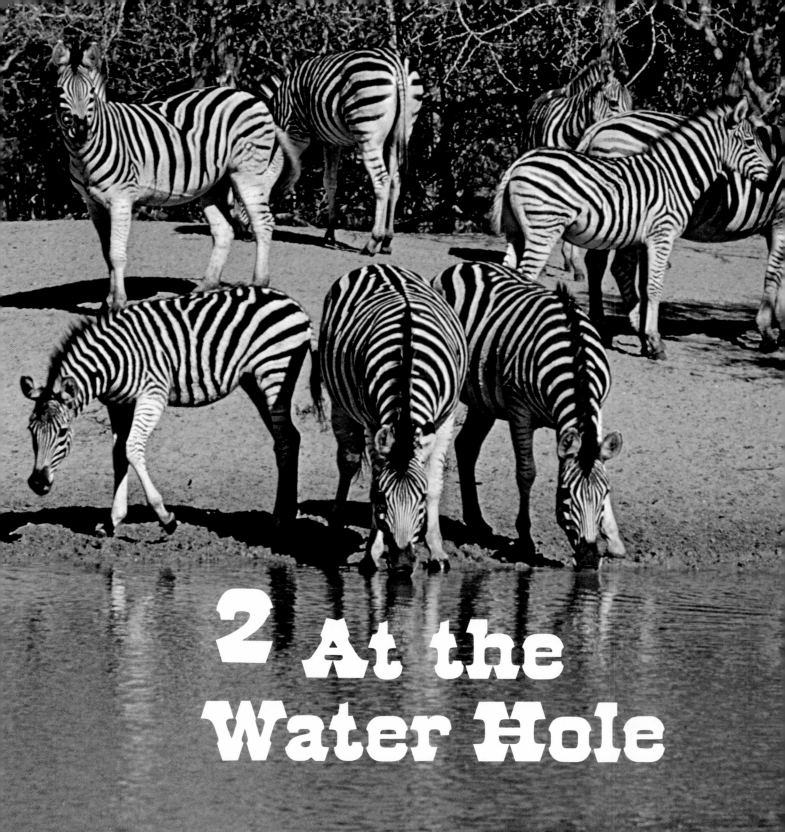

2 At the Water Hole

Wherever they live in Africa, zebras are part of a community of other wild animals. Some, like antelopes, share the open plains. Others, such as leopard and rhino, roam forest or bush country. Their life styles are as different as their coats, but the local water hole is a meeting ground. All of them must have water to live.

Come then to the water hole and see what happens this day. Come in the last cool hours of the fading night. Hide yourself in the thicket close by and wait for dawn and the animals of woods and plains.

Here's one fellow now, grown bold by the growing daylight. His spiralling horns, polished by nature, are long and gracefully curved. They shine in morning's pink glow.

He's a buck impala, an antelope. Behind him follow his hornless does. Their big, liquid eyes search the "pan," the muddy hollow that the rainy season has filled with water. Their ears, twice as long as a hare's, listen for any sound of movement. A leaf crunches, and off the impalas race. But they'll be back.

At midmorning a giraffe arrives, rocking gently as he trots to the edge of the basin. Slowly, he twists his neck, and with eyes that can see far-off things, he scans the horizon. He takes his time. It is better not to hurry. There may be trouble afoot.

A wildebeest, then impalas drink (below).   **Finally, it's zebras' turn (opposite).**

Then he saunters close, spreads his long legs, and swings his head. Up and down it goes, three times, four. His nose touches the faintly rippled pool. He drinks; moves on.

The air grows hot and quiet, except for the buzzing of flies. You wait impatiently, wishing for more visitors. And all at once your wish is granted.

Here they come, a troop of monkeys turning high noon at the water hole into a circus. Baboons, dozens of them, burst on the scene, racing, romping, squabbling. Toughies argue over who drinks first, then off they go, a band of gypsies enjoying a carefree life on the plains.

A zebra stallion arrives, leading his herd through the nearby woodland of thorny acacia trees. They move cautiously, stopping often to look and listen. Even a snapping twig could send them stampeding.

But before they reach water's edge, slate gray wildebeests crowd round the hole. They are clumsy-looking antelopes with scraggly beards and thin legs. The graceful impalas have returned and wait on the bank above. On the far side of the pan, tracks of other animals tell of visitors during the night or early

Wildebeests, with crescent-shaped horns, dip to slake their thirst.

dawn. The paw prints of a leopard mark the water's edge. A rhino has churned the mud as he wallowed.

The zebras wait their turn. Just then, a bird flies out of a tree with a startled screech. He has spied danger and given the first warning. The wildebeests charge from the water, zebras wheel and take flight. Impalas vanish with soaring leaps. Within seconds, the water hole is deserted except for a butterfly that drops to the water for an instant.

The bird has seen lions. Now a pair of them pad from the bushes to lap thirstily. They move lazily, their stomachs plump with last night's dinner. Then the zebras and all the other animals know that there is nothing to fear.

Even before the lions have gone, three zebras troop back to the water's edge. More crowd in, nipping and shoving. They are untidy drinkers and churn the water into waves.

When the zebras leave, a few late-comers take their place. But as dusk shadows the thickets, fewer plains animals arrive. They fear ambush from enemies . . . leopards and other creatures of the night. So let us, too, pad softly away.

Meanwhile, other antelopes, fleet-footed impalas, wait patiently.

21

Under long-legged mother
a newborn giraffe finds
security and protection.

3
Growing...
Up!

Little flecks of milk dotted the corners of Jaro's mouth, for he had just finished nursing. He was only four hours old. He leaned sleepily against his mother's shoulder.

Young as he was, Jaro was taller than any zebra. He was over five feet high from round hoofs to fuzzy ear-tips. His sixteen-foot-tall mother stood above him like a giant.

Jaro's first days were lazy and carefree. His whole world was a woodland of flat-topped acacia trees where his mother nibbled leaves while he tagged along. Jaro's mother watched him closely, not letting him wander. She knew she had only lions to fear for herself, but for Jaro there were other predators, animals eager to run him down. One day, hungry hyenas came slinking around Jaro when he strayed too far. No mammal has better eyesight than a giraffe, so Jaro's mother quickly saw the danger. She sped to Jaro, and soon had him tucked between her long forelegs. If a giraffe must fight, it will. Jaro's mother had huge cloven hoofs, and enough power to easily pound the hyenas to bits. They did

Necks swinging, a cow, young bull, and calf gallop across the plains.

not dare come near the little one.

Jaro grew fast. In a week he was a sturdy six-footer. A pair of tiny horns were hardening into bone under their covering of skin and hair. He was a Masai giraffe, a kind with brown leafy splotches. Jaro's were much paler than his mother's.

When he was two weeks old, Jaro met some of the other giraffes in the world. He was frisking behind his mother as she led him through the trees. Not looking where he was going, he butted into the rump of a strange giraffe. Startled, he stared

24

up. It was a female, or "cow" of his mother's herd. She leaned down with big friendly eyes. Jaro saw other giraffes, too. Some were calves, like himself. It was a "nursery" herd of cow giraffes and their young. The big males, or "bulls," kept to themselves most of the time. Occasionally one would wander over to play nursemaid and round up the little ones.

Jaro and his mother lived with the nursery herd from that day on. She began to pay less attention to him, often wandering away for hours. It did not matter. Other cows took care of Jaro. Young giraffes become independent early in life, although they go to their mothers to nurse until they are about nine months old.

Jaro watched the adult giraffes strip acacia leaves from branches with tongues eighteen inches long. Acacias are thorny, but the giraffes did not mind. Thick, gummy saliva protects their mouths.

Soon Jaro began nibbling leaves. He chose a small tree, just his height. Delicious! He ate more and more, enjoying his new food.

Trips to the water hole were great adventures, but the older giraffes

**◄Legs splayed, baby bobs for salt.
A cow twists to chomp a branch. ►**

25

were so jumpy. They did not like lowering their heads to drink because it gave hungry lions such a good chance to attack. But they always kept a sentinel on guard.

Jaro had much to see and learn. Older bull calves in his herd were often sparring in a special, peculiar way of male giraffes. It is called "necking." First, they would stand shoulder to shoulder, shoving. Then they began swinging their necks, first back, then to the side. A giraffe's neck is *not* stiff. It can bend almost like rubber. The young bulls tried to hit each other's bodies with their heads. As bull giraffes grow older, their heads grow heavy with layers of bone. Older bulls can even knock each other out with their mighty head blows.

The giraffes knew all the neighborhood lions. They knew when they were hunting. They knew when they were only loafing about with full bellies. It is hard for a lion to surprise a giraffe—but sometimes they do. One quiet afternoon, a lion did stalk close to Jaro. It moved to spring. One snapping twig gave the lion away, just in time. Instantly, the whole giraffe herd broke for the open plains, Jaro in their midst. A giraffe's long legs can carry it along at thirty-five miles per hour. It can outrun a horse. The lion lost his chance for a meal as Jaro and his herd galloped off rapidly, across the wild grasslands of Africa.

◄**Adult bulls fight by "necking."**
The sentinel scans the horizon.►

SAVING THE LAND OF THE ZEBRA

What will happen to Africa's wildlife if you build a superhighway through the land of the zebra? Africa will soon find out.

The Transafrican Highway is being built now through Equatorial Africa. When completed, the highway will run 4,400 miles from coast to coast—cutting through savanna, tropical forest, mountain, and desert—and will link Lagos in Nigeria to Mombasa in Kenya.

The concrete road will do no harm. It follows paths used for many years. But what will the road bring? Hope-

fully, there will be new cities, new towns, and a new way of life for all.

If this happens, will there still be a place for the zebras, the giraffes, and the other animals of Equatorial Africa? Young people in groups that meet to study wildlife are determined that there will be.

Kenya's wildlife clubs were launched in 1968 to make people aware of Kenya's natural wealth and, especially, her remarkable wildlife. Similar clubs have sprung up in other African nations. Some clubs are for future teachers, some for high school students. Some, like the "Chongololo Clubs" of Zambia, are for youngsters in elementary school.

Through the clubs, young people are learning new things about their country and how to handle its resources wisely. But how does a six year old or a sixteen year old come to care about a gazelle he has never heard of or a giraffe he has never seen in the wild, or perhaps not even in a zoo?

He reads books, hears lectures, watches films. Best of all, he goes out into the field and sees the live ani-

Plump zebras and graceful hartebeests enjoy the rich bounty of the savanna.

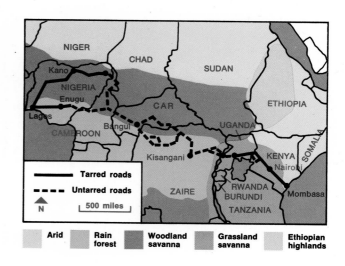

Out of old roads, widened and extended, the Transafrican Highway will be born.

mals roaming forest and plain.

Don't you wish you could take a weekend in paradise and see the giraffe, tallest animal on earth, nibbling on thorny acacias, or an elephant scraping his tusk on a baobab tree?

The youth of Africa are coming to know these and other animals and why they are important: they are Africa's pride. They also bring money as tourists come to see what is surely the greatest show on earth.

If the wildlife here or anywhere is to be saved, land for the wildlife must be saved. If today's leaders forget this, you, the leaders of tomorrow, must remind them.

WHERE ZEBRAS AND GIRAFFES LIVE

ZEBRAS in great masses once galloped over all of Africa's savannas. Today, large herds graze on the wet plains and in the grassy woods of central, eastern, and southern Africa.

30

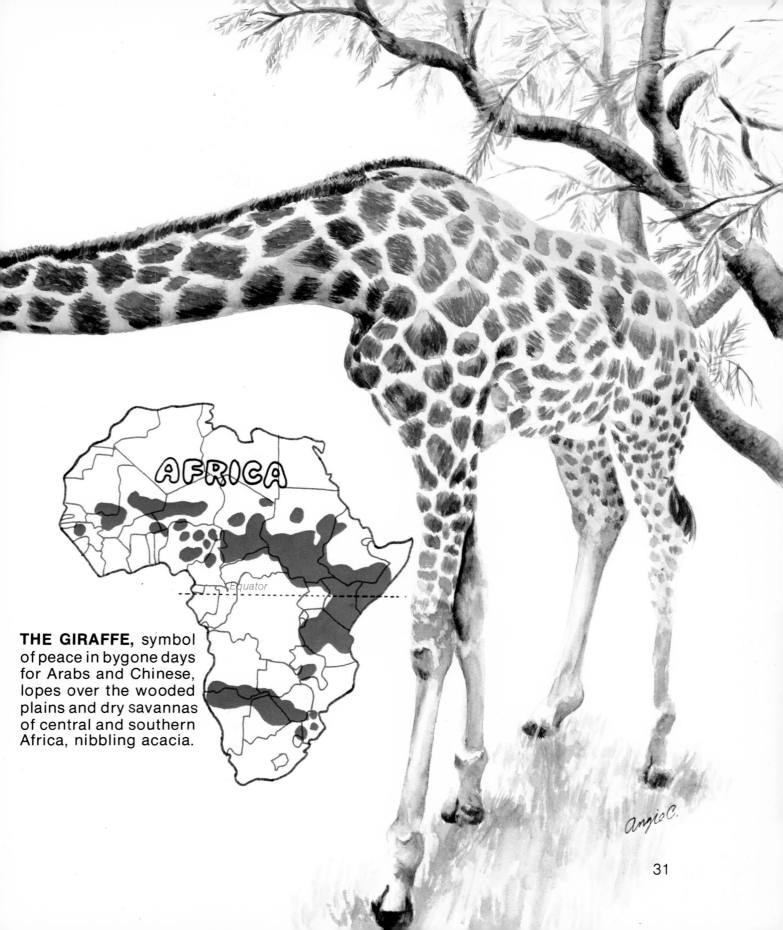

AFRICA

Equator

THE GIRAFFE, symbol of peace in bygone days for Arabs and Chinese, lopes over the wooded plains and dry savannas of central and southern Africa, nibbling acacia.

AngieC.

31